My Piano, My Body and Me

making the most of two wonderful machines

Richard Smith

Book 1
early grades

eye for ideas®

My Piano, My Body and Me

With Many Thanks & Much Love to my wife Mary and our wonderful family

Copyright © 2015 Richard W. Smith All rights reserved.

First edition printed 2015 in the United Kingdom

A catalogue record for this book is available from the British Library.

ISBN 978-0-9575012-4-9

Richard Smith has asserted his right under the Copyright, Designs and Patents Act 1988 to be identified as the composer and author of the music and text in this book.

No part of this book shall be reproduced or transmitted in any form or by any means, electronic or mechanical, including photocopying, recording, or by any information retrieval system without written permission of the publisher.

Published by Eye for Ideas, 1, Bownham Park, Rodborough Common, Gloucs., GL5 5BY

For more copies of this book, please e-mail; **info@eyeforideas.com**

Cover and layout by The Creative Consortium, Stroud GL5 4AQ

Printed by 4edge Limited, 7a Eldon Way, Eldon Way Industrial Estate, Hockley, Essex SS5 4AD

Although every precaution has been taken in the preparation of this book, the publisher and author assume no responsibility for errors or omissions. Neither is any liability assumed for damages resulting from the use of the information contained herein.

With Many Thanks to my good friends Linda Pegrum, Julian Hellaby, Richard Reason and my son Aidan for generously giving their time to make such incisive and immensely helpful observations.

My Piano, My Body and Me
making the most of two wonderful machines
Book 1 - early grades
Richard Smith

Contents

Contents	main focus	
My Piano (Part 1)		2
Beginnings	interpretation	3
My Piano (Part 2)		4
Beginnings (complete version)	dynamics	5
My Body (Part 1)		6
Blue Shades	legato; dynamics	7
My Body (Part 2)		8
Little Chinese Junk	staccato	9
My Body (Part 3)		10
Waltz of the Echoing Cuckoo	"Drop-Slur"	11
Me - My Mind (Part 1)		12
Daydreaming	legato & cantabile	13
Me - My Mind (Part 2)		14
A Chordial Welcome!	playing chords	15
Me - My Mind (Part 3)		16
Pebble in Deep Water	indirect pedalling	17
Left Handed Rag	hands working independently (balance)	18
On Tenterhooks	hands working independently (staccato & legato)	19
Two Timing Boogie	hands working independently (ties)	20
Crown & Sceptre	hands working independently (melody & countermelodies)	21

eye for ideas®

My Piano, My Body and Me
My Piano - what is this wonderful musical instrument?

A piano is a large mechanical dulcimer.

What is a dulcimer?

A dulcimer is very much like a xylophone except that the wooden bars are replaced with strings. As with a guitar or violin, these are stretched over a sound board to amplify the sound. The player strikes the strings with hammers or mallets in each hand.

How is a piano mechanical?

Instead of striking the string with a hammer the pianist strikes a key which operates a series of levers which causes the hammer to hit the string.

Immediately afterwards the hammer drops away so that the string can continue to vibrate, as in the diagram.

This unit of key - levers - hammer is duplicated for every black and white note on the piano, so typically there are 88 identical sets of them on each instrument!

Why are there around 88 notes on a modern piano?

The notes go step by equal step from the lowest pitch to the highest that the human ear can commonly distinguish.....so even if there were notes which went higher or lower (and on some pianos there are), most people would not be able to hear the difference!

The person generally credited with this inspirational innovation is Bartolomeo Cristofori (1655 - 1731) who invented and refined his mechanism in Florence from 1700. Its full name is **pianoforte** (**piano** means 'quiet' in Italian; **forte** means 'loud'); it was the first keyboard instrument which could sound loud or quiet depending on the force with which the player strikes the keys. Before this their dynamic range was restricted; a **clavichord** is quiet compared with an organ or harpsichord. An **organ** does have a swell pedal to vary the volume but its application is quite different. Playing keys lightly or heavily on a **harpsichord** does not make it sound softer or louder. Keyboard music written before this time (e.g. by J. S. Bach and D. Scarlatti) accordingly contains very few expressive directions. The next generation of composers started to make increasing demands on manufacturers to produce more expressive instruments.

What are the piano's characteristics that a pianist can control?

Not as many as you might think! In addition to playing **quietly or loudly**, a pianist can also control **how long a note sounds**. The note stops sounding when the finger is lifted from the key. If the key is held down, the sound dies away naturally; the lower the note, the longer the sound lasts, because a long string continues to vibrate for a greater time than a short one.

Play and hold down the highest note on the piano. Listen how quickly the sound fades. Now do the same with the lowest note and notice how it continues for a longer time.

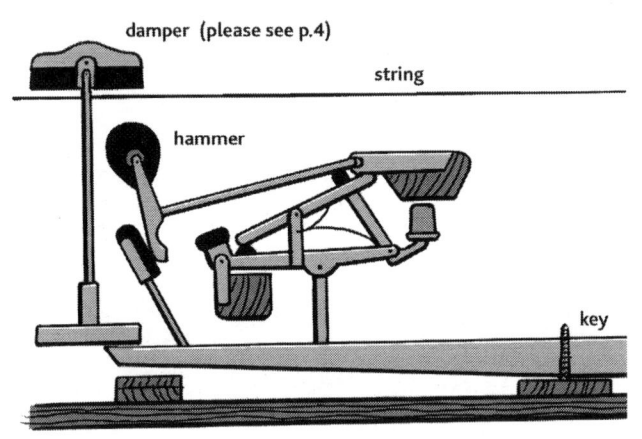

Beginnings

A vital part of a musician's job is to interpret the music. What do you think the composer is wanting to say? How can you best express this when you play the piece? There are no phrase marks here, nor indications how fast, slow, loud or soft to play. Should it get louder or quieter in certain places, faster or slower? If so, where? Does the piece call for any pauses, perhaps just before the end? How about fingering? It is up to the performer to decide. There are some suggestions over the page.

Richard Smith

The character of a piano's sound can be varied by the pedals. The right hand (sustaining) pedal controls **the dampers**. These are the small felt pads which rest above the strings in a grand piano (as in the diagram overleaf) and *between* (slightly below) the hammers and the strings on an upright. On both instruments the dampers are in contact with the strings until the sustaining pedal is depressed, which moves all the dampers away so that the strings can vibrate freely. When the pianist lifts the foot from the pedal, the dampers return to their original position and once again deaden the sound of the strings.

Conclusion

With relatively few variables available, a pianist needs to use the whole body to extract as much as possible from the instrument, which leads us to the next section.

Exercise

Despite these apparent limitations, the piano is very expressive and a favourite solo instrument for many composers. How would you interpret these sounds on the piano?

a) climbing upstairs;

b) birds flying and singing;

c) thunder & lightning.

Many composers have written piano music based on man made and natural sounds. Listen to Debussy's Preludes 'The Sunken Cathedral' ('La Cathédrale Engloutie'), 'Fireworks' ('Feu d'Artifice') and Daquin's 'The Cuckoo' ('Le Coucou') for example.

What is the difference between a grand and an upright piano?

Both types work in similar ways, resulting in hammers hitting strings. In an upright piano the workings are vertical so that it occupies less floor space. However this limits the length of the longest string. In a grand piano, the horizontal workings enable manufacturers to make instruments in different lengths.

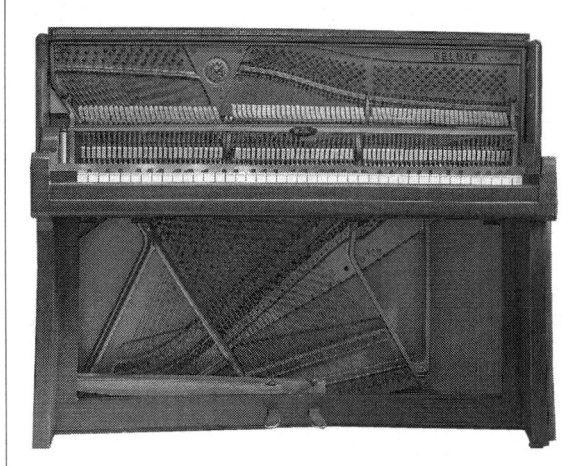

There are commonly three names used to describe the size of a grand piano:

1. a baby grand is the smallest, in which the strings may even be shorter than those on a typical size upright piano;

2. a boudoir grand has longer strings which generally give a richer, rounder sound;

3. a concert grand is the largest (a typical instrument is 2.7 metres - 9' - long), generating the massive sound associated with a concert hall.

Dynamics (p.12)

Beginnings

There is no right or wrong way to interpret a piece; it is up to the performer to decide. Here are some suggestions.

Richard Smith

My Piano, My Body and Me
My Body

If a pianist only has limited control over the volume, duration and character of the sound it is vital to make the best use of every part of the body to get the most out of the piano.

How and where should you sit at the piano?

There is no 'right' or 'wrong' way, something which works for one person may be unsuitable for another. However, to allow your body to perform at its best on the piano, **a pianist must learn to relax** at the keyboard. This means no uncontrolled tension in the body muscles; more about this below.

Do I need a piano stool or will a chair do?

A piano stool has no back, may commonly be adjusted for height and has a flat, upholstered seat. This allows a pianist to sit comfortably upright and still reach easily up and down the keyboard. Most chairs and some stools have a back, are often too high or low and cannot usually be adjusted, are inclined forwards or backwards and are contoured to the shape of the body. All these factors restrict movement, so the answer is 'yes' a piano stool is essential for the serious pianist.

How far should the stool be placed from the piano?

It should be opposite the middle of the keyboard, at a distance from the keys so that the player may comfortably reach the highest and lowest notes without having to bend excessively, as in the diagram. In relation to this bird's eye view, the arms and wrists should keep as straight and as close to a right angle with the keyboard as possible; more of this later.

From the side (please see the diagram below) the elbows and wrists should be a little higher than the keys; this improves the pianist's overall control. There are some occasions when it is beneficial to lower the elbows and wrists but the higher position should be the default one.

Sit at the keyboard like this:

Many musicians practise *The Alexander Technique*, devised by F M Alexander in the late 19th century and much of this section is based on this. The intention is to obtain the greatest return from the least effort. Sit at the edge of the stool to minimise friction (but not so that you slip off!) This enables the player to reach all the keys, including the highest and lowest, with ease.

Of course what works well for one may not work for another and there is no single correct answer. Pianists sit in the same position for some time so **it is important to sit comfortably**.

The bottom should feel well supported by the stool. As you sit, your SITTING BONES are situated at the base of the spine above the top of each leg. These should be fully and comfortably accommodated on the stool, so that THE HEAD LEADS UP and the whole torso follows; neck, shoulders and back.

Feet comfortably on the floor

Legato (p.14); Dynamics (p.12)

Blue Shades

All the notes in this piece fall within a five finger pattern in each hand so there is no need to look down at the keys. It does however need a sensitive legato touch with particular consideration to dynamics and the final rit.

Listen particularly to the left hand when it is accompanying the tune in the right hand to make sure it remains in the background then let it stand out when it plays the short melodic passages in bars 7 - 9 and 13 - 16.

Andante con moto

Richard Smith

Copyright © 2015

The Upper Body

Look towards the music rather than down at the hands. This encourages playing by touch, allowing the player to focus on the music which makes sight reading easier. **'Don't Look at the Keys!'** also available from *eye for ideas*, develops the technique of playing by touch.

The muscles in the neck, shoulder and back **should be free of tension**. Let the arms, elbows, wrists and hands **relax**.

When you have to play demanding musical passages the back muscles often become tense, so let your body **remember how this relaxed state feels and retrieve it** at such potentially stressful times.

The Feet

Ignoring the pedals at this stage, the **whole length of both feet** should be able to rest comfortably on the ground. If the pianist is not tall enough to do this, place a foot stool at a height which allows both feet to be placed firmly on it with no tension in the ankles. This enables the pianist to play in relaxed comfort with elbows and wrists above the keyboard (see also **pedalling** on page 16).

The Hands

Let both hands fall naturally down the sides of the body like a rag doll; imagine you have strings tied round your wrists like a puppet. Now pretend that a puppeteer is pulling the strings and let your hands and arms drop above the keys of the piano, as in the diagram.

Shake them about to make sure they are floppy and loose. Then let your wrists gently down on the keys so that your relaxed fingers play them but your wrists control the height.

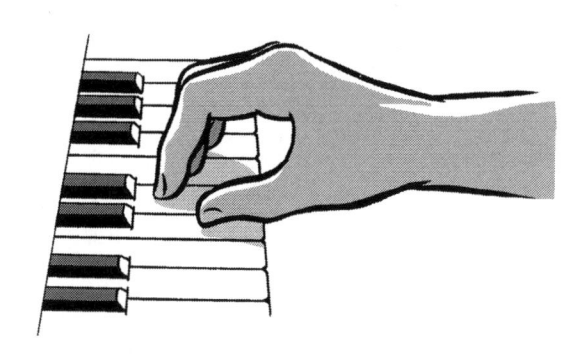

This should be the position to which you naturally return although there are times when you need to tense the fingers and joints to play a particular passage (e.g. 'subito' on page 14).

Three Points to Ponder

1. There is a great temptation to strike the keys **hard**; please resist it! A gentle touch should be the norm, keeping something in reserve both quieter and louder, to play *f* and *p* passages effectively.

2. It is similarly tempting to play pieces **faster** than you can comfortably control! This too is unnecessary. It is more satisfying for you and much more attractive for your audience to hear an accurate and sensitive rendition of the piece rather than a fast one. As above, play comfortably within your ability so that you remain in control for any accelerando passages, but equally able to avoid rallentando passages becoming dreary!

Staccato (p.14)

Little Chinese Junk

Please remember to relax your arms and wrists as you play this piece. Start by playing bars 5 & 7, i.e. with quavers in both hands, at a speed with which you are comfortable, then let this set the pulse for the whole piece.

Richard Smith

3. From a bird's eye view (as in the top diagram on page 6), please remember to keep your **elbows and wrists as close to a right angle** with the keys as you comfortably can when playing at the top and bottom end of the piano. There are times when this is not practical but you can improve the situation by leaning slightly to the right or left and back a little; it will allow your hands and fingers to keep closer to 90 degrees. The benefits are that the fingers are less likely to slip off the black notes or strike a wrong note, as well as encouraging relaxation and control.

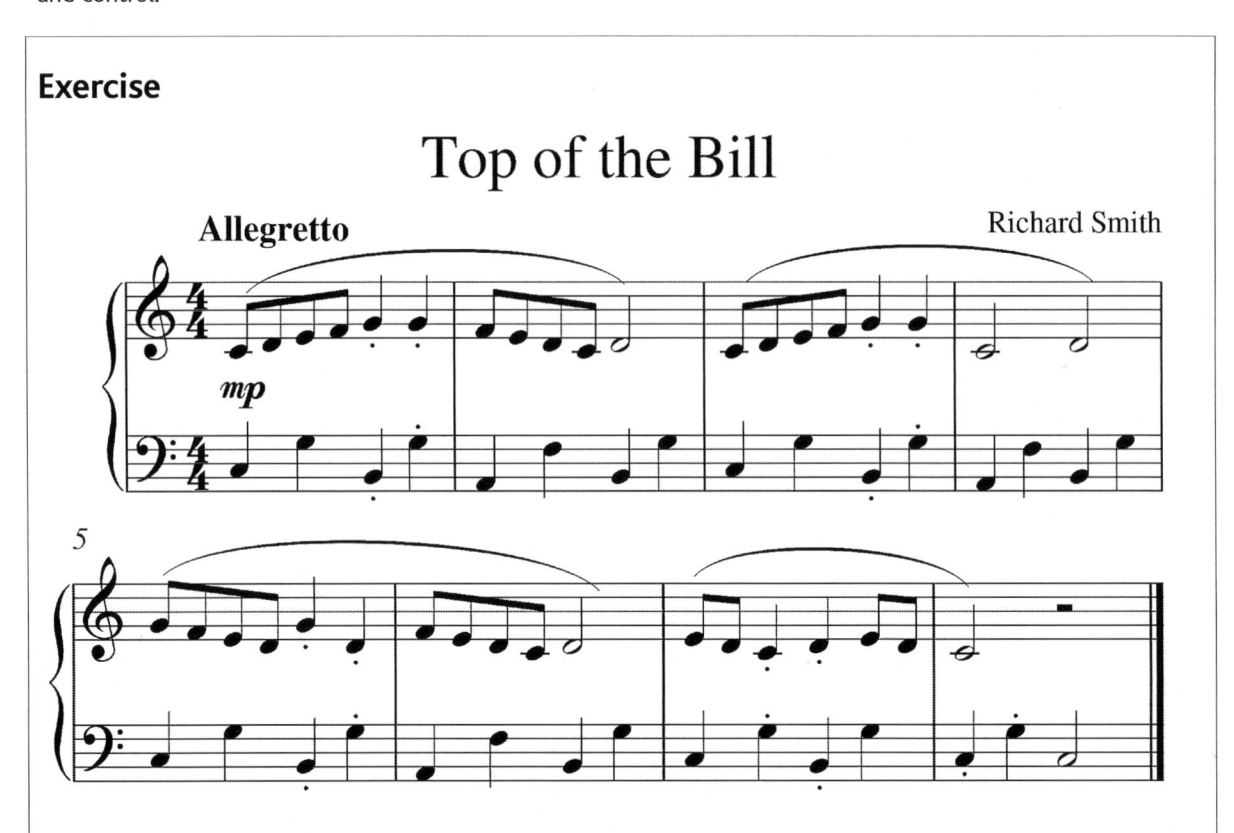

Exercise

Top of the Bill

Richard Smith

Allegretto

mp

Play this piece as written, listening as you play. Then play it with both hands two octaves lower, noting how this changes its character. Play it at the top of the piano (three octaves higher than written) and listen to the effect.

The Bottom Line

Richard Smith

Adagio

mp

Play this as written and listen to the sound. Now play it at the top end of the piano; note how the high notes fade quicker than the low ones. This is the reason that dampers are not needed for the highest strings on a piano.

Play it two octaves lower than written and listen to the resonance of those bottom notes.

See how both pieces sound with the piano top open; then with the pedals down, first the una corda (left) one, then the sustaining pedal and notice the different effects created.

Briefly, the una corda pedal works in different ways on upright and grand pianos with slightly different results, but the general effect is to make the sound mellower. It will be covered in greater detail in a later volume of **'My Piano, My Body and Me'**.

'Drop-Slur' (p.14); Hands working independently (p.16)

Waltz of the Echoing Cuckoo

Just as the two syllables in the word 'cuckoo' are as loud as each other, so the two notes in a 'drop slur' should have equal volume, neither 'CUC-koo' nor 'cuc-KOO'. A relaxed wrist will help to achieve this.

Think about the balance of the hands from bar 25, the right hand can easily drown out the left.

Richard Smith

My Piano, My Body and Me
Me - My Mind

Your mind can now instruct your body to make the most of this wonderful instrument.

If all that a pianist can vary is **how long** the notes are held, **how hard** they are struck and their **sound quality** (if the pedal is used), then it is vital to have a very clear idea **from the outset** of the interpretation that he or she is seeking to achieve.

Music is above all an emotional experience for the player and the audience; a musical journey with the performer as guide. The responsible navigator will have a vision of the destination - where the piece is going, how it gets there and the metaphorical sights to be seen along the way.

So it is not only the composer's ideas that are paramount, the pianist must have an interpretation in mind for the performance to have a meaning.

So **before you play a piece,** think about the way in which you will play it - **loud, quiet, getting louder or quieter in certain places** (if so, where and how loud or quiet?)

Try playing **'Top of the Bill'** (p.10) loudly. Now try it softly. Which do you prefer? Try getting louder, then getting quieter.

Play the eight notes of the scale each louder than its predecessor to hear eight steps of different volume. Then reverse the exercise starting loudly, getting quieter. This will help to decide how loudly or quietly to play a piece, retaining something in reserve for quieter or louder passages later on.

It also highlights how the body can influence the way a passage is played. Because the fingers have different strengths a note played by the thumb for example, may be played unintentionally louder than one played by finger four because the thumb is naturally stronger. This should be borne in mind particularly with *cantabile* passages when certain notes may need emphasis regardless of which fingers are playing them.

Think about the **tempo**. Unless there is a metronome indication as well, the speed of *Adagio* and *Allegro* is approximate and at the discretion of the performer.

'Beginnings' (p.3) has neither dynamic nor tempo indications, so have a look, play around with it and work out for yourself how you would like it to sound. The piece is repeated on page 5 with the composer's suggestions.

1. loud & quiet; crescendo & diminuendo; practise 'Beginnings' (p.5); 'Blue Shades' (p.7)
As was explained earlier in 'My Body', relaxation especially in the shoulders, elbows and wrists is the secret to playing sensitively, loudly as well as quietly; *crescendo* and *diminuendo*.

If you have trouble deciding on an interpretation of a piece, try **playing the opposite to the instructions in the music;** loud instead of soft and vice versa. This will give very strong indications how you think it ought to sound.

Please bear in mind that your audience probably perceives your performance louder than you do, so if in doubt play softer than you think the piece needs. If a loud passage is coming up, play a slight *diminuendo* in the passage immediately beforehand; it will make the *forte* more effective.

In a similar way a deliberate *ritardando* can have a comparable effect to a *crescendo*, so the real *crescendo* can be saved for the climax.

Legato and cantabile (p.14); hands working independently (p.16)

Daydreaming

Practise the long cantabile passages separately without the left hand, listening to make sure that the phrasing is smooth and the melody sings out; effective fingering is vital.

Richard Smith

Allegretto Cantabile

2. legato and cantabile; practise 'Blue Shades' (p.7); 'Daydreaming' (p.13); 'A Chordial Welcome' (p.15); 'Left Handed Rag' (p.18); 'On Tenterhooks' (p.19); 'Two Timing Boogie' (p.20); 'Crown & Sceptre' (p.21)

For a really smooth *legato*, **listen to what you are playing**. Only lift the finger off the note that is sounding when you play **and hear** the next note so that the second note follows the first with no gap. For an effective *cantabile*, let the phrase swell louder then quieter (or the other way round), still maintaining the *legato*.

As stated above, for longer phrases make sure that notes played by your stronger thumb do not sound louder, especially when it passes under your hand in a scale passage, or your weaker fingers are crossing over your thumb to play. Scale practice (especially hands separate) is particularly useful in this regard.

Let the last note of a phrase sound fractionally shorter to create a brief pause before the first note of the next phrase, like a comma in written prose or a breath in speech.

Silence is golden! Daniel Barenboim said that every piece starts and ends with silence. Mozart said that **rests are as important as notes** for a delicate interpretation. For the same reason there is no reason to hurry over pauses.

3. staccato; practise 'Little Chinese Junk' (p.9)
Tutor books often ask students to imagine that the keys are glowing red hot, burning the fingertips if they are left there too long. Staccato passages are played by bouncing your fingertips on the keys to make them sound short and stopped - but listen to what you play **to achieve the desired volume and pressure on each key**. Avoid the risk of striking the wrong note by lifting your wrist or fingers too high. Once again, relaxed wrists and arms make for a consistent sound and secure playing at a steady pulse.

Staccato is not just the note, but also the silence after it (see above); it is neither always fast nor loud! To play softly use a light, controlled touch **with a combination of finger and wrist** to maintain a quiet sound. Start with a simple staccato scale playing one hand at a time, listening as you play.

4. 'drop-slur'; practise 'Waltz of the Echoing Cuckoo' (p.11)
The 'drop-slur' is two notes sounding EQUALLY LOUD or QUIET, the first is played *legato* with the second which is stopped short, *staccato*. The hand and arm movements come from a relaxed wrist where the weight of the finger on the key causes the note to sound.

5. subito; practise 'Crown & Sceptre' (p.21)
Flick the **wrist** for a sudden *forte* sound; let the **wrists absorb the weight of the arm and hand** to achieve a sudden *piano*. The fingers and hand should remain relaxed throughout.

6. playing chords; practise: 'A Chordial Welcome' (p.15); 'Pebble in Deep Water' (p.17); Crown & Sceptre (p.21)
It is easy for one note in a chord to sound inadvertently louder than the others. Make sure also that the fingers strike the notes **together** and not one slightly before the other. As you play, **listen** for any unevenness. Start by playing bar one of **'A Chordial Welcome'** on page 15 aiming for a smooth *legato*. Move to bar two for similar practice with the left hand. Even though the piece does not demand it, try playing the chords *staccato*. It is essential that the wrist flicks the whole hand so that the notes sound equally loud or quiet and for the same short length of time.

Bars three and four introduce the need to hold one note slightly longer while the thumb plays consecutive notes. Practise these two bars first then bars five and six to achieve this smoothly with either hand.

Playing chords (p.14); legato (p.14)

A Chordial Welcome!

Practise bars one and two (separately and together) to get used to playing a sequence of legato chords.

The four rising legato chords in bar 3 (left hand) and 5 (right hand) are challenging as the thumb has to play two consecutive notes which inevitably disrupts the smoothness of the phrase. To minimise this let the finger playing the other note in the chord (left hand finger 3 playing F#, right hand finger 2 playing B) hang on to its note as long as possible without disrupting the pulse. Only lift that finger off the note when you hear the next chord sound. This is as close to true legato as nature will allow!

Richard Smith

Copyright © 2015

7. hands working independently; practise 'Crown & Sceptre' (p.21); also 'Waltz of the Echoing Cuckoo' (p.11); 'Daydreaming' (p.13); 'Left Handed Rag' (p.18); 'On Tenterhooks' (p.19); 'Two Timing Boogie' (p.20)

At first it can be challenging to play differently in each hand, e.g. loud in the right, quiet in the left or vice versa; perhaps *staccato* in the left, *legato* in the right. With practice it gets easier! Try playing the scale of C major hands together, *staccato* in the right hand, *legato* in the left. Play it slowly at first, AS SLOW AS NECESSARY TO ACHIEVE THE DESIRED EFFECT. Gradually you will be able to speed up. Then swap over and play *legato* in the right, *staccato* in the left. You will discover that you can concentrate one part of your brain on one side of your body, while the other side works almost by itself and I think it is immaterial whether you are ambidextrous, left or right handed.

The same principle applies when playing tied notes in one hand, sometimes creating syncopation, as in ragtime, boogie-woogie and much of pop music.

To bring out a particular passage in one hand which is also having to play other (harmony) notes at the same time, **incline the wrist** and move that part of the hand nearer the keys so that the fingers playing the inner melody can emphasise the part more effectively as in the diagram.

8. legato (indirect) pedalling; practise: 'Pebble in Deep Water' (p.17)

The sustaining pedal raises the dampers on a piano so that all strings resonate together, adding their harmonic sounds. It is sometimes called the 'loud' pedal but this is incorrect because the notes are no louder; a broader sound is created and it lasts longer but the volume is unaffected.

When using the pedal, the ball of the foot should not leave its surface, while the heel is kept firmly on the floor.

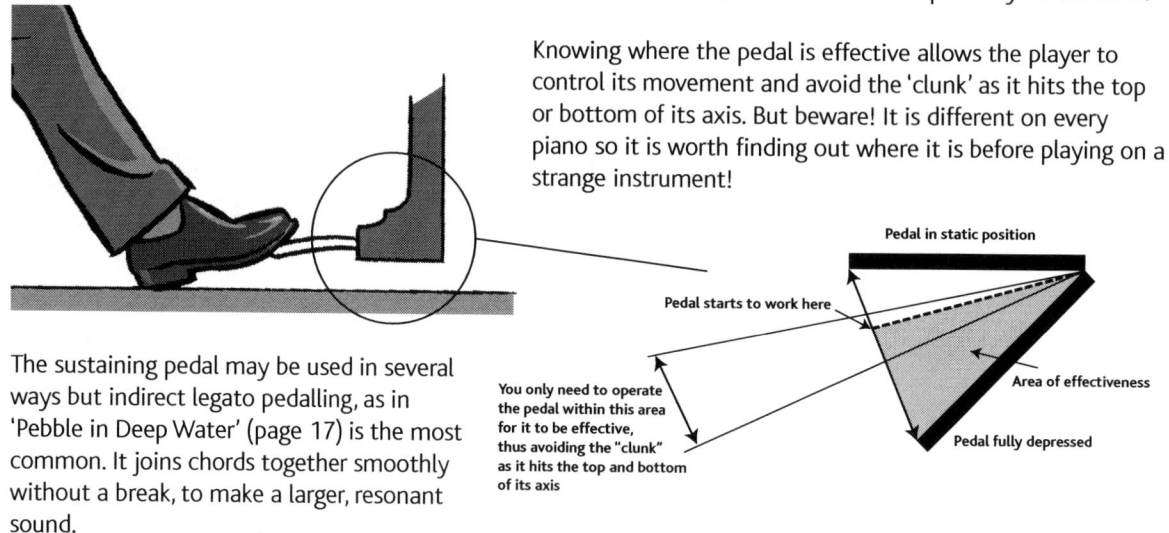

Knowing where the pedal is effective allows the player to control its movement and avoid the 'clunk' as it hits the top or bottom of its axis. But beware! It is different on every piano so it is worth finding out where it is before playing on a strange instrument!

The sustaining pedal may be used in several ways but indirect legato pedalling, as in 'Pebble in Deep Water' (page 17) is the most common. It joins chords together smoothly without a break, to make a larger, resonant sound.

You only need to operate the pedal within this area for it to be effective, thus avoiding the "clunk" as it hits the top and bottom of its axis

Pedal in static position
Pedal starts to work here
Area of effectiveness
Pedal fully depressed

The pedal is depressed AFTER a chord is played but while the keys are still being held down. Raise it and depress it again to clear the sound, perhaps at a change in harmony or as directed in the music.

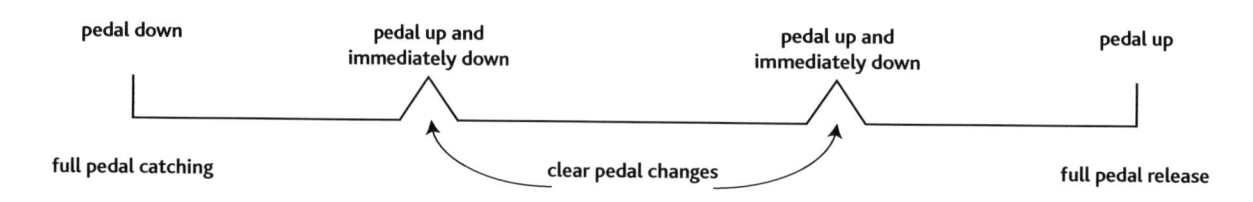

pedal down | pedal up and immediately down | pedal up and immediately down | pedal up

full pedal catching | clear pedal changes | full pedal release

Indirect pedalling (p.16); playing chords (p.14)

Pebble in Deep Water

This is a slow, relaxed piece to practise using the sustaining pedal. The una corda (left) pedal may also be used to create a soft, mellow sound. Note the effect created by playing staccato quavers while holding down the sustaining pedal.

In these passages please listen to ensure that the split between left and right hands does not affect the sound.

Richard Smith

Adagio molto rubato e espressivo

Legato (p.14); hands working independently (p.16)

Left Handed Rag

Effective fingering is as important as a relaxed wrist to achieve a smooth left hand legato. The phrases are unequal in length; make short 'breaths' between them by shortening the last note of each.

Listen also to the chords in the right hand to balance the tune with its accompaniment.

Richard Smith

Allegretto

Hands working independently (p.16); legato and cantabile (p.14)

On Tenterhooks

Richard Smith

Hands working independently, including ties (p.16); legato and cantabile (p.14)

Two Timing Boogie

To practise hands working independently, start by playing the left hand minims by themselves and set up a rocking motion: this will soon become almost automatic. The right hand is then ready to add the syncopated tune. Reverse the practice when the hands swap roles.

Moderato

Richard Smith

Hands working independently (p.16); legato and cantabile (p.14); playing chords (p.14)

Crown & Sceptre

Richard Smith

Maestoso con moto

rit.

Copyright © 2015

More inspiration from eye for ideas®

Don't Look at the Keys!
978-0-9575012-3-2

a progressive set of imaginative pieces inspiring confidence to play the piano by touch; to encourage musical playing and fluent sight reading. The technique is clearly explained at the start, together with simple, enjoyable exercises and a short section for teachers suggests how to use the book in lessons and for students at home.

for young composers (& their teachers)
978-0-9575012-1-8

a practical guide to start writing music and reassuring reference for those supporting;

for GCSE Music students and teachers, ABRSM Theory and the composition option in Trinity/Guildhall examinations. Students create their own music from the start, exploring rhythm, melody and expression. The book covers film and incidental music, simple harmony and musical form. Additional material supports teachers throughout, the whole written in easily accessible language, presented in an attractive format.

Crazy Crotchets & Quirky Quavers
978-0-9575012-2-5

wacky action piano duets, as much fun to perform as they are to watch!

Players swap places, appear to get in each other's way, play with an orange, or a rag (why else are pieces called 'Rags'?) & more; Liven up piano lessons, recitals and school concerts! Elementary & Beginner Grades.

for more information
please contact **info@eyeforideas.com**

www.eyeforideas.com
Eye for Ideas, 1 Bownham Park, Rodborough Common, Gloucs, GL5 5BY